Stargazer's Alphabet

Night-Sky Wonders from A to Z

John Farrell

BOYDS MILLS PRESS

HONESDALE, PENNSYLVANIA

Acknowledgments

The author would like to thank Dr. David Turner,
professor of astronomy and physics at Saint Mary's
University, Halifax, Nova Scotia, Canada, for his
assistance in making this book possible. Thanks also
to Rosanna Hansen for her thoughtful guidance,
helpful suggestions, and encouragement.

Image Credits
Akira Fujii/David Malin Images: front cover, p. 3 (background), 6 (Andromeda night sky), 7, 8, 9, 16,
17, 18, 19, 20, 21 (bottom), 22, 24, 25, 28–29 (background); NASA Marshall Space Flight Center
(NASA-MSFC): p. 1, 6 (Andromeda galaxy), 8–9 (background), 12, 12–13 (background), 15, 20–21
(background), 26; NASA and the Hubble Heritage Team (STSci/AURA): pp.6–7 (background), 16–17
(background), 24–25 (background); Courtesy of NASA, *Apollo 8* Crew: pp. 4–5 (background), 10–11
(background); The Astronomy Students at Amtsgymnasiet and EUC-Syd, Denmark: p. 11; Courtesy of
W. Liller and IHW/LSPN and NSSDC/NASA: p. 13; NASA/JPL/PIRL (Planetary Image Research
Laboratory)/University of Arizona: p. 14; Courtesy of NASA/JPL/Table Mountain Observatory.
Photographer: James W. Young, resident astronomer: p. 21 (top); NASA, J. Bell (Cornell University)
and M. Wolff (SSI): p. 23 (Mars); *THEMIS Public Data Releases*, Mars Space Flight Facility, Arizona
State University, (2006) http://themis-data.asu.edu: p. 23 (Echus Chasma); Courtesy of NASA Glenn
Research Center at Lewis Field: pp. 22–23 (background); Courtesy of NASA/Ames Research Center,
Artist: Rick Guidice: p. 27 (surface of Venus); Illustration by Tom Powers: p. 27 (greenhouse effect);
NASA NSSDC Pioneer Venus Orbiter: pp. 26–27 (background); NASA/CXC/SAO/S, Murray M.
Garcia: p. 29; NESDIS/National Geophysical Data Center: pp. 30–31 (background).

Boyds Mills Press, Inc.
A Highlights Company
815 Church Street
Honesdale, Pennsylvania 18431
Printed in China
www.boydsmillspress.com

Library of Congress Cataloging-in-Publication Data

Farrell, John.
  Stargazer's alphabet : night-sky wonders from A to Z / John Farrell.
    p. cm.
  ISBN-13: 978-1-59078-466-2 (alk. paper)
  1. Astronomy—Observers' manuals. 2. Stars—Observers' manuals.
  3. Constellations—Observers' manuals. I. Title.

QB63.F37 2007
520—dc22

      2006020029

First edition, 2007
The text of this book is set in 13-point Sabon.

10 9 8 7 6 5 4 3 2 1

To my family and our singing and stargazing friends on Prince Edward Island, who enrich many summer nights with music and a shared sense of wonder

—J.F.

Introduction

As a boy, I enjoyed looking up at the stars. I remember how excited I got one time when I found the Big Dipper above the house of our neighbor, Mr. Wells. Years later, as a teenager, I sat with friends around a campfire near the ocean. The sky overhead was filled with twinkling stars. I couldn't see Mr. Wells's house, but I did find the Big Dipper above the sand dunes, and I was delighted to know it was there. For a long time the Big Dipper was the only star pattern I knew, but over time my curiosity led me to books and teachers who helped me learn about the night sky.

As an adult, I've spent countless hours studying the Moon, looking at the stars and planets, and watching meteor showers. It's a great thrill for me when I'm able to help someone see a certain pattern in the stars, identify one of the planets, or find the Andromeda Galaxy for the first time. I find it exhilarating when two or more people I'm with see the same meteor and gasp or call out at the same time, "Did you see that one?"

For many years now, I have gone out to look at the sky nearly every night, and I'm seldom disappointed. I still feel that same sense of awe and wonder I felt as a beginning stargazer. I hope this book will help you find your way around the night sky and that you, too, will experience the joy and excitement of discovery.

Our Place in Space

If you look up at the night sky on a clear evening, you can see thousands of stars. Some are bright and easy to spot, others less bright, and others so faint you can barely see them. One thing they all have in common is that they appear as tiny points of light, even when you look at them through a telescope. The stars look small because they are very, very far away.

But if you could see them close-up, they might look something like our Sun, which is also a star. Since the Sun is so close, it looks much bigger and brighter than any other star.

Earth is a planet. There are other planets, too, such as tiny Mercury and giant Jupiter. Each of them travels around the Sun in a path called an orbit. Comets, asteroids, and meteoroids orbit the Sun, too. They are also part of our solar system.

The Sun belongs to a huge group of more than 100 billion (100,000,000,000) stars that make up our great galaxy, which we call the Milky Way. Our galaxy is big, but the rest of the universe is much bigger. Astronomers think that the part of the universe we can see with today's telescopes contains more than 125 billion galaxies.

When people looked at the night sky long ago, they saw patterns among the stars. Some patterns looked like animals or objects. Others were thought to stand for the heroes and gods of myths. Today, we call these star patterns constellations.

As your guide, this book will help make your starry explorations awe-inspiring and fun. So turn the page, and let's find out more about stargazing from *A* to *Z*!

When to Look

This book gives the best times to see a number of interesting objects in the night sky. On the dates given, look for the objects from nightfall until about midnight. Because of Earth's rotation, the view of the sky changes throughout the night. The objects described may not be in view after midnight.

Where to Look

Use the Sun to find north, south, east, and west. The Sun rises in the general direction of east each morning and sets in the west at night. Once you know where east and west are, you can find north and south. When you stand with east on your right and west on your left, you are facing north. To look south, simply turn around.

A is for Andromeda, our neighbor galaxy.

THE ANDROMEDA GALAXY is the largest galaxy near our Milky Way. Even though the Andromeda galaxy is a neighbor, it is still more than two million (2,000,000) light-years away. Use binoculars or a telescope to look for this small, cloudy patch of light.

● **Andromeda**
an-**DRAW**-mih-duh

▶ **What Is a Light-Year?**
A light-year is the distance light travels in one year—about six trillion (6,000,000,000,000) miles.

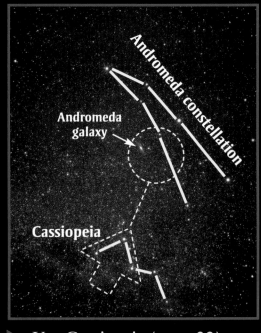

Andromeda constellation

Andromeda galaxy

Cassiopeia

▶ Use Cassiopeia (page 22) to find the galaxy.

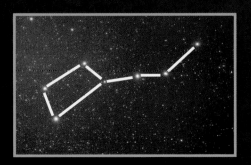

B is for the Big Dipper, that's an easy one to see.

THE BIG DIPPER is easy to find. Its stars are bright, and it looks like a dipper or ladle. Look for it in the northern evening sky all year long. But because of the motions of the Earth throughout the year, the Big Dipper always seems to be on the move.

The Big Dipper is part of a constellation named Ursa Major, which means "Great Bear" in Latin.

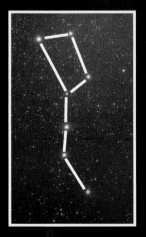

March

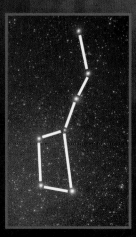

July

May

C is for Cygnus, flying through the Milky Way.

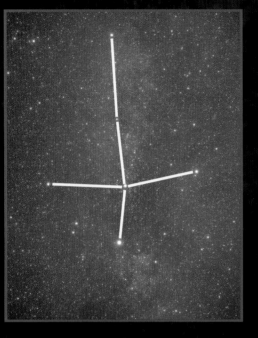

Cygnus
SIG-nus

IN DEEP TWILIGHT in late August and early September, the brightest stars of the constellation Cygnus form the outline of a cross floating high overhead. This star pattern, or asterism, is known as the Northern Cross. As the sky grows darker, more stars appear. The full pattern looks like a flying swan. Look for Cygnus in the night sky from springtime through autumn.

Draco
DRAY-koh

D is for Draco,
a dragon on
display.

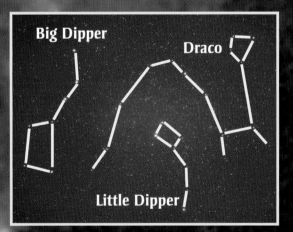

Big Dipper

Draco

Little Dipper

THE CONSTELLATION DRACO covers a large area of the northern sky and is highest in midsummer. Using this diagram, start by finding the dragon's boxlike head, high in the northern sky. Look for two faint stars and two brighter ones. You'll see that the tip of Draco's tail lies near the cup of the Big Dipper. This shape is similar to that of a dancing dragon used in Chinese New Year celebrations.

E is for Earth, our mother ship in flight.

DID YOU KNOW that Earth moves as fast as a spaceship? Earth zooms around the Sun at about 67,000 miles per hour in a path called an orbit. It takes Earth one year to go around the Sun one time. The force of gravity keeps Earth in its orbit—and keeps us from flying off Earth.

This famous photograph was taken by the crew of the Apollo 8 *spacecraft as they orbited the Moon on December 24, 1968. They were the first people to see Earth from so far away.*

F is for the first star that you wish upon at night.

This photo shows the brilliant planet Venus.
Venus sometimes appears close to the horizon in the west soon after sunset. At other times it is low in the east just before dawn, but it never appears overhead. If the first bright, "star-like" object you see is low in the sky, it is probably Venus. If the bright object is overhead, it may be Jupiter.

Star light, star bright,
First star I see tonight,
I wish I may, I wish I might
Have the wish I wish tonight.

OFTEN THE FIRST "STAR" people wish upon at night is not a star at all but a planet—usually Venus or Jupiter. Stars give off their own light because they make their own energy and are much brighter than any planet. But these two planets look brighter than the stars because they are much closer to Earth and because they have wide surfaces that reflect a lot of sunlight.

G is for our galaxy, a pinwheel made of stars.

THE ANCIENT GREEKS called our galaxy the Milky Way because they thought the narrow, hazy band of light stretching across the sky looked like spilled milk. When we see the Milky Way, we are looking into the edge of the flattened disk of our galaxy. The whole Milky Way contains more than 100 billion (100,000,000,000) stars.

 From far away our Milky Way galaxy *would look something like this one. It has a pinwheel shape because it is spinning.*

H is for Halley's Comet, which visits from afar.

COMETS are mountain-sized balls of ice and rock that orbit the Sun. When a comet comes close to the Sun, the Sun's energy blasts away some of its icy body. That's when we see a bright patch of light with a spectacular tail of dust and gas, which can stretch for millions of miles. The famous Halley's Comet can be seen once every seventy-six years, and will return in 2061.

Halley rhymes with *Sally*.

I is for Io,
an astronomer's delight.

● **Io**
EYE-oh *or* EE-oh

IO IS THE MOON closest to Jupiter. This moon is about the same
size as Earth's Moon but otherwise is very different. Io's surface rocks
are colorful. Scientists think they are deposits of lava and sulfur from
Io's many active volcanoes. You can see Jupiter's four biggest moons,
including Io, with powerful binoculars or a small telescope. These
objects are called the Galilean moons after the Italian scientist Galileo
Galilei, who discovered them in 1610.

J is for mighty Jupiter, the ruler of the night.

IN ROMAN MYTHS, Jupiter was the king of the gods. In the night sky, Jupiter is the king of the planets. This giant world is more than 88,000 miles across at the equator. That's more than eleven times wider than Earth. Jupiter's clouds are driven by wind speeds as fast as 400 miles per hour. Through a small telescope you can see the Great Red Spot—the top of a storm that has been raging for nearly four centuries.

K is for the Kite—Boötes is its name.

BOÖTES WAS A HERDSMAN in Greek mythology. His constellation looks like a kite and appears in the evening sky from spring through early autumn. The brightest star in the constellation is brilliant Arcturus, which marks the bottom of the kite. To find Boötes, first find the Big Dipper, then follow the curving path of the handle away from the Dipper's cup to bright orange Arcturus. Remember: "Follow an arc to Arcturus."

■ **Boötes**
boh-OH-tees

■ **Corona Borealis**
kuh-ROH-nah bore-ee-AL-is

★ **Arcturus**
ark-TOOR-us

▶ Corona Borealis ("the Northern Crown") is a smaller constellation next to Boötes.

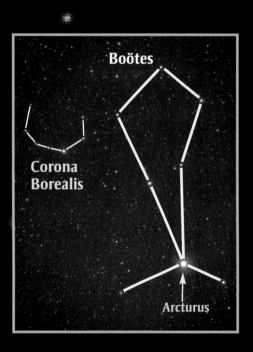

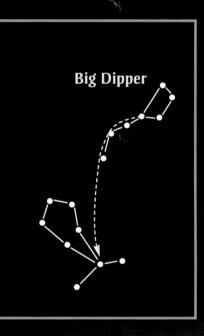

16

L is for the Lion, who has a starry mane.

LEO THE LION is visible from February through June. Look for a large backward question mark. This shape includes six stars and makes the outline of Leo's mane and chest. Then look a little to the east (left) and you'll see a triangle of three bright stars—Leo's hind end and tail. The star at the bottom of the backward question mark is the brightest star in this constellation. It is called Regulus, from the Latin word for "prince."

★ **Regulus**
REG-you-luss

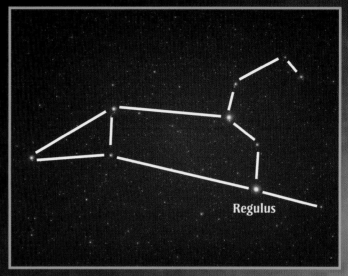

Regulus

A great time to see Leo is in April, when it hangs overhead about two hours after sunset.

M is for Earth's Moon, which causes tides to ebb and flow.

Site of the *Apollo 11* landing and humanity's first steps on the Moon.

EARTH'S GRAVITY keeps the Moon in orbit around Earth. But the Moon also tugs at Earth with its own weaker gravity. When one side of Earth faces the Moon, the Moon pulls on the ocean there, raising the tide to its highest level. In fact, the Moon also pulls Earth away from the ocean on the far side. That makes a second high tide on the opposite side from the Moon.

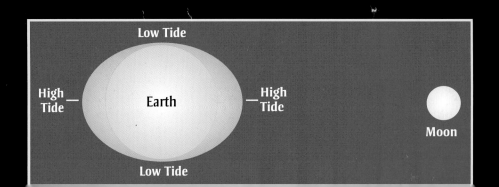

Low Tide

High Tide — Earth — High Tide

Moon

Low Tide

N is for the North Star, which guides travelers as they go.

SINCE ANCIENT TIMES, travelers have used one special star to find the way North. Of all the stars in the sky, only the North Star always stays in

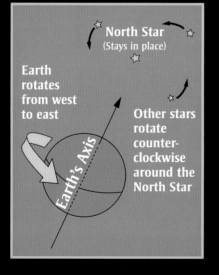

North Star
(Stays in place)

Earth rotates from west to east

Other stars rotate counter-clockwise around the North Star

Earth's Axis

the same place. The rotation of Earth on its axis makes all other stars appear to move across the sky. But the North Star lies directly above the axis. That's why it seems fixed in the sky while all the other stars wheel around it.

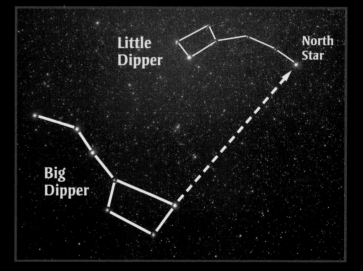

Little Dipper

North Star

Big Dipper

To find the North Star and the Little Dipper, draw a straight line out from the first two stars forming the cup of the Big Dipper. The first bright star you come to is the North Star. It is the last star in the handle of the Little Dipper.

O is for Orion, whose belt is straight and bright.

WHEN ORION APPEARS, winter is near. This hunter from Greek mythology wears a belt made up of three bright stars. A line of fainter stars curves down from the belt, forming a sword. If you look at the sword through binoculars, you will see that one of the "stars" is really a fuzzy patch of light. It's not a star at all. It's the Orion Nebula, a cloud of gas and dust where stars are being born.

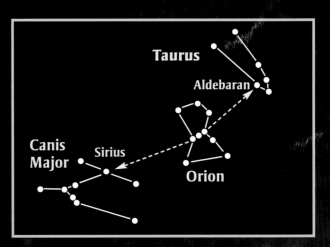

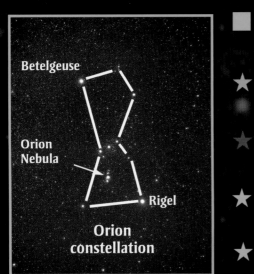

Orion
oh-RYE-un

★ **Rigel**
RYE-jul

★ **Betelgeuse**
BEE-tul-JOOS

★ **Sirius**
SEER-ee-us

★ **Aldebaran**
al-DEB-a-rahn

Use Orion's belt as a pointer to two other bright stars: Sirius and Aldebaran. The belt stars point to the left to Sirius, in the constellation Canis Major, the Greater Dog. To the right, the belt leads to the reddish eye of Aldebaran, in Taurus the Bull.

The constellation Perseus is not shown in this photograph of a meteor.

THE PERSEID METEOR SHOWER

occurs each August when Earth passes through a trail of dust left behind by a comet called Swift-Tuttle. Meteors form when bits of this dust plunge into Earth's atmosphere. As each bit of dust falls through the air, it rubs against air molecules. The heat of friction vaporizes the dust, making a streak across the sky.

 **Perseid**
PURR-see-id

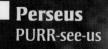 **Perseus**
PURR-see-us

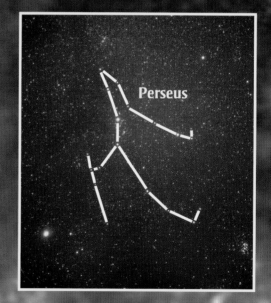

The Perseid meteor shower got its name because its meteors appear to streak outward in all directions from the constellation Perseus, which rises around midnight in the northeastern sky during August.

21

Q is for Queen Cassiopeia, upon her throne of stars.

■ Cassiopeia
(KA-see-uh-PEA-uh)

Cassiopeia lies in the north all year. In summer, it looks like the letter W. In winter, it resembles an M. These shapes don't look much like a queen. But in spring, when the M is on its left side, we can imagine that it's a throne.

THE MYTH OF CASSIOPEIA has been told in many ways. Here is one version. Queen Cassiopeia bragged that she was more beautiful than the sea nymphs. This angered Neptune, the ruler of the sea. To punish Cassiopeia, he sent a sea monster to attack the coast of her country. Cassiopeia and her husband offered their daughter, Andromeda, as a sacrifice to the sea monster. The hero Perseus rescued her.

Summer   **Winter**   **Spring**

R is for the Red Planet, the one that we call Mars.

THE ROCKS AND SOIL on Mars are rich in iron oxides, or rust. That's what makes the planet red. NASA has sent robots to explore Mars and spacecraft to orbit it. These exploring machines found clues that water might have once flowed on Mars. Since water is necessary for life, that discovery is a sign that life might have existed on the Red Planet.

Channels that look like riverbeds are evidence that Mars once had water.

S, the Summer Triangle, tells us when summer's here.

THE SUMMER
TRIANGLE is a star
pattern, or asterism,
formed by three bright
stars: Vega, Deneb, and
Altair. The triangle
signals the coming of
summer when it appears
in the east in mid-June.
Each of the three stars in
the triangle is the
brightest star in its own
constellation.

★ **Vega**
(VAY-guh)

★ **Deneb**
(DEH-neb)

★ **Altair**
(al-TAIR)

▪ **Lyra**
(LIE-ruh)

Cygnus
(SIG-nus)

▪ **Aquila**
(ah-KWILL-uh)

T is for Taurus, which shines when winter nights are clear.

A V-SHAPED PATTERN OF STARS outlines the face and horns of Taurus the Bull. The giant red star Aldebaran stands as one of the bull's eyes. Use Orion (page 20) to find Aldebaran in late fall and early winter. On clear nights, the V shape is easy to find.

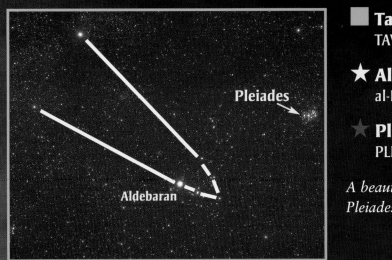

■ **Taurus**
TAW-rus

★ **Aldebaran**
al-DEB-a-rahn

★ **Pleiades**
PLEE-uh-deez

A beautiful cluster of stars called the Pleiades floats above Taurus the Bull.

U is for the universe— that's everything there is.

The universe is full of galaxies. In this image alone, there are more than 10,000 galaxies, yet the picture shows only a tiny patch of sky.

MOST ASTRONOMERS believe the universe emerged from a huge explosion of energy called the Big Bang. When the Big Bang happened, the universe expanded outward, creating space and all the galaxies within it. Today, we still see the galaxies rushing away from one another. Based on the galaxies' speed, astronomers think the universe is close to 14 billion (14,000,000,000) years old.

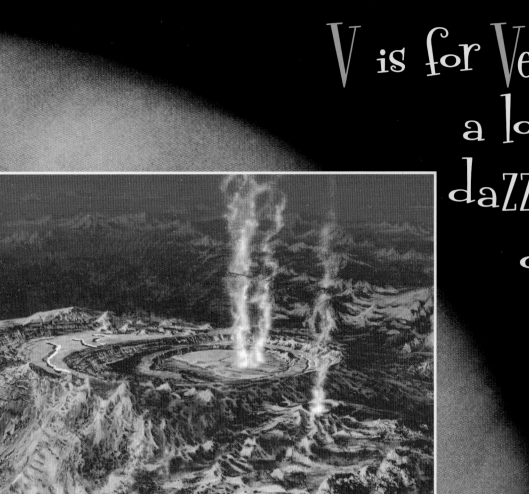

THE ANCIENT ROMANS named this bright planet after their goddess of beauty. But the surface of Venus is hardly beautiful. It is covered by lava plains, huge volcanoes, and mountain ranges. The planet is blanketed by clouds of carbon dioxide that trap heat from the Sun. These clouds give Venus a runaway greenhouse effect. The planet holds in so much of the Sun's energy that its surface is hot enough to melt lead.

See page 11 for a photograph of Venus on the horizon.

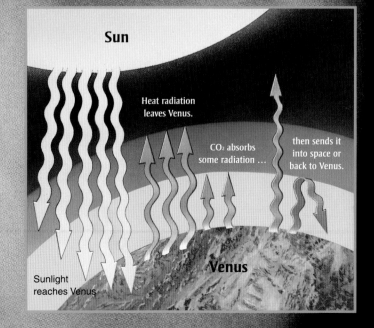

Sun

Heat radiation leaves Venus.

CO_2 absorbs some radiation ...

then sends it into space or back to Venus.

Sunlight reaches Venus

Venus

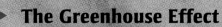

▶ **The Greenhouse Effect**

W is for the wonders that await us in the night.

WHEN YOU GO STARGAZING, choose a clear night when the Moon is not full. Before you go outside, pick some constellations and stars from this or other sky-watching books so you can recognize them in the sky. A star wheel, or planisphere, is also a great way to learn the constellations. Just remember, you won't be able to see all the constellations all the time.

X is for exquisite and extraordinary sights.

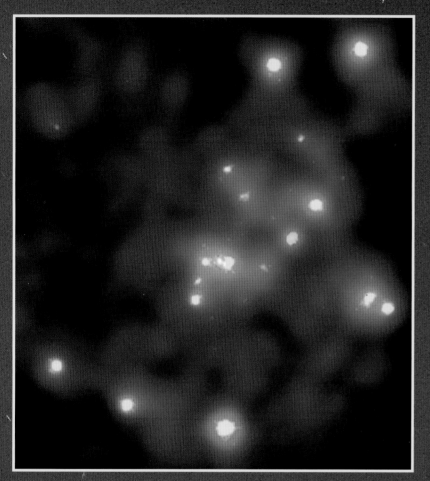

TO SEE some extraordinary sights, we need telescopes that detect X-rays. A black hole is a dead star with gravity so strong that nothing is fast enough to escape from it, not even light. How could we ever find a black hole? As bits of material fall into a black hole, they rub together. Friction makes the material so hot that it gives off X-rays. So a faraway object that gives off X-rays is likely to be a black hole.

NASA's Chandra telescope took this picture of the X-rays coming from the Andromeda Galaxy. The blue dot in the middle is a giant black hole at the center of the galaxy.

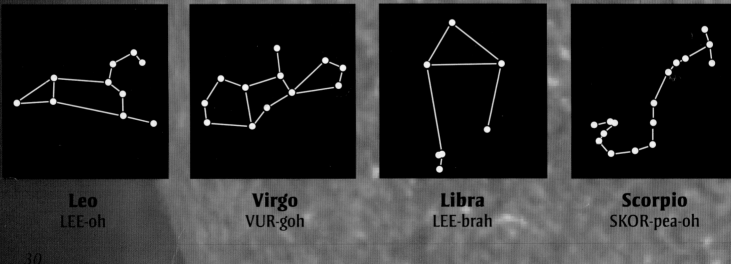

Y is for the yellow stars, like our own great Sun.

WHEN YOU LOOK UP at the night sky, most stars look white. But they actually have different colors. A star's color shows how hot it is and how much energy it is giving off. The hottest stars are blue. White stars are the next hottest, followed by yellow stars like our Sun. Red stars are the coolest of them all. Rigel is a blue star, and Betelgeuse is red. Both are in Orion (page 20).

Astronauts in a space shuttle orbit Earth at more than 17,000 miles per hour. At that speed, it would take them more than seven months to reach our Sun, which is more than 93 million (93,000,000) miles away.

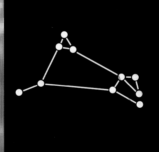

Aries
AIR-ees

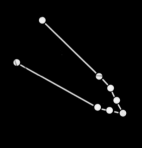

Taurus
TAW-rus

Leo
LEE-oh

Virgo
VUR-goh

Libra
LEE-brah

Scorpio
SKOR-pea-oh

Z is for the Zodiac—
now our alphabet is done.

THE ZODIAC is an imaginary band across the sky that contains twelve constellations: Aries, Taurus, Gemini, Cancer, Leo, Virgo, Libra, Scorpio, Sagittarius, Capricorn, Aquarius, and Pisces. These star patterns lie along the path that the Sun, Moon, and most of the planets follow as they move across the sky.

This concludes our alphabet of astronomy. As you set out on your own star-gazing adventures, you will discover that the night sky contains a bounty of even more wonders from *A* to Z.

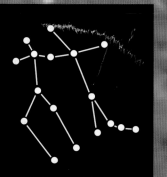

Gemini
JEH-mihn-eye

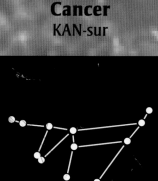

Cancer
KAN-sur

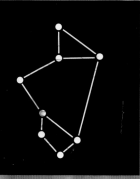

Sagittarius
SAJ-ih-TAIR-ee-us

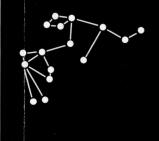

Capricorn
KAP-rih-korn

Aquarius
uh-KWAIR-ee-us

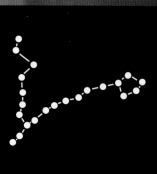

Pisces
PIE-seez

Glossary

asterism a pattern of stars that is not a constellation.

asteroid a world that orbits the Sun as the planets do but is much smaller.

astronomy the scientific study of space and everything in it.

axis an imaginary line upon which an object such as a planet rotates.

Big Bang a huge explosion that occurred about 14 billion (14,000,000,000) years ago. Scientists think the Big Bang was the beginning of the universe as we know it.

black hole a star that ran out of fuel and collapsed under the force of gravity to the size of almost nothing. The pull of gravity creates a space from which nothing is fast enough to escape, not even light.

comet an icy object that develops a tail of gas and dust when its orbit takes it close to the Sun.

constellation a star pattern that may represent a person, a god, an animal, or an object from ancient myths.

galaxy a giant group of millions to hundreds of billions of stars.

greenhouse effect the warming of a planet caused by carbon dioxide and other gases that prevent heat from escaping into space.

light-year the distance light travels through space in one year, about six trillion (6,000,000,000,000) miles.

meteor a streak of light caused by a meteoroid vaporizing as it falls through Earth's atmosphere.

meteorite a meteoroid that hits Earth because it does not completely vaporize as it falls through the atmosphere.

meteoroid a piece of rock, dust, or other matter that can enter Earth's atmosphere and vaporize as it falls, creating a meteor.

Milky Way the galaxy that includes our solar system.

moon a rocky world that orbits another world. The word comes from the name for Earth's Moon.

myth a traditional story involving gods, goddesses, and heroes that often explains natural wonders.

mythology a collection of myths from one people. Many objects in the sky are named after characters in Greek or Roman mythology, but other peoples also named constellations after characters in their own mythologies.

nebula (plural: **nebulae**) a cloud of gas and dust. Some nebulae are the birthplaces of stars. Planetary nebulae are the remains of stars that exploded.

orbit the path that a planet, moon, or other object follows as it goes around another object.

planets large objects that orbit the Sun, such as Earth, Jupiter, and Mars.

planisphere a device that shows the stars that can be seen at a given time on a given night.

solar system the Sun and everything that orbits it.

star a large ball of gas that gives off light and is held together by the force of its own gravity.

star wheel see **planisphere**.

Sun the star at the center of our solar system.

tide the rising or lowering of ocean waters caused by the pull of gravity from the Moon or Sun.

universe all matter and energy that exists.

X-ray high-energy light that cannot be seen by the unaided eye.